# DOG STORIES

Deanna—
Thank you so much
for your kind words.
God Bless—

Published in the United States by 14 Hands Press

www.14handspress.com

Library of Congress subject headings

Camp, Joe

Dog Stories/ by Joe Camp

Dogs, Life, Self Help

The Soul of a Horse: Life Lessons from the Herd

ISBN 978-1-537115-48-1

First Edition

Our cover girl is Sadie Camp

# DOG STORIES

#### EVERYTHING YOU NEED TO KNOW ABOUT LIFE IS RIGHT THERE AT YOUR FEET

## JOE CAMP

14 HANDS PRESS

My previous books explored our journeys with horses, and movies, even dog training. But I woke up one morning and realized that after so many years of making movies about a dog, and living with dogs, and loving dogs, I had never stopped to explore the impact these dogs have had on my life and the choices I have made. This book is written to rectify that omission because the effect of that impact has been profound.

*Joe Camp*

*For all the dogs in the stories that follow.*

# CONTENTS

Prologue  1

1. Forget the Neighbors  7

2. Just Do It  13

3. Are You Listening?  19

4. Never Look Back  27

5. Dig Until You Find It  33

6. Wheels Do Turn  41

7. Lead, Follow, or Get Out of the Way  51

8. Every Rule Has Its Exceptions  57

9. Fido in the Boardroom  65

10. They Do Know Best  71

11. Ugly  79

# PROLOGUE

Did you know that folks who have suffered a heart attack have an eight times better chance of surviving the first year if there is a pet in the house. That's a measured and documented fact. Those with pets also have fewer doctor visits, lower heart rates, lower blood pressure and cholesterol, shorter hospital stays, and an easier time recuperating after an illness. What the authors of this amazing new research aren't quite sure of is *why*.

We know why, of course. Those of us who have lived with dogs all our lives. We know what the nuzzle of a wet nose under our palm, looking for a scratch on the head, can do to an elevated stress level. The medical community is only now catching up.

But it goes deeper.

Dogs know more than we do.

By knowing less.

They realize that one's soul prospers from sharing, caring, relating, fulfilling. And they know there is nothing more important in life than love. Not money. Not status. Not peer pressure.

Nothing can make you feel better than doing something good for somebody else. Putting another being before yourself. Not cars. Not houses. Not facelifts. Not watching television.

When I come home there is nothing that will stop Benji from being at the front door to announce with a happily dancing tail: *I am so happy you're home. I love you. Touch me, scratch my head, look for a moment into my eyes and we'll both feel better. I know it. I promise.*

And we both do. Instantly.

And so does the rest of the family, because in that one moment all the grisly little trolls of stress or angst or worry or hurry who are grappling and scratching at my insides suddenly start gagging and losing control, evaporating back into their moldy caverns where they belong. Left is a fuzzy warm glow that forcibly twists the corners of my mouth into a wee smile of contentment. Whether I want it to or not.

Love. It's amazing stuff.

I've spent three decades wandering around inside the heart and soul of a dog, writing Benji stories, directing Benji movies, trying to understand how to better draw you, the audience, in there with me. To cause you to feel the pain and joy of a dog's experiences. Fortunately for me, and I hope for you, there's been another benefit. The time and effort spent on four legs learning to inhale the world from a canine point of view has taught me many amazingly simple lessons about life. Lessons that can and should apply to *our* lives, yours and mine, because they work better.

Dogs, in fact, do know best.

If you don't have a dog, or two, or three, there's no way for you to understand this concept, much less embrace it. So put this book down immediately and go straightaway to your local animal shelter. Don't open the cover again until you have a warm puppy or a big old lab sprawled in your lap. Then you'll be welcomed back with open arms.

Or if you're already convinced that I'm certifiable, in need of therapy, you might choose now to bail because it only gets worse from here.

For the rest of us, those who have dogs, squeeze in closer for a moment and ponder this quiz. Have you ever told a little white lie? Or maybe a bigger one that wasn't even white? Have you ever stomped through the front door all grumpy and barking at your kids, or your spouse? Have you ever questioned the value of being persistent, not giving up? Or being loyal? Or having passion? Have you ever had to work at making someone else happy? Have you ever shaded the truth in a business deal? Or pondered the meaning of the word *selfish*?

Your dog hasn't. None of the above.

And we can all learn from that.

And that's what this book is about.

*Joe Camp*

When is the last time you went outside and laid
in the grass with your tongue hanging out?"

*Annonymous*

# 1

## FORGET THE NEIGHBORS

Have you ever really watched your dog? I mean *really* watched? And thought about what might happen to your life if you did exactly what he did? With the same exuberance? If you incorporated a bit of your dog's daily routine into your own life?

Sound silly? I decided to spend a day doing just that. Observing my dog and copying everything he did. Well, okay, it didn't wind up being a full day. And, no, I didn't copy *everything*. I chose, for example, the house bathroom over the tree in the front yard. And I filed away until later the challenge of digging up to my elbows into a gopher hole. But so much of the experience was just amazing. I could actually feel my usual morning blood pressure dropping.

Of our five dogs, for this experiment, I chose Shaggy because he's a dog of the moment. The tiniest things make him delirious. If ever a dog stopped to smell the roses, it's Shaggy.

First thing out the door, he stopped, lifted his nose to the sky… and sniffed. A lot. Not letting any of the morning smells get past him. I tried it. Closed my eyes and sniffed the morning. Tried to take it all in. It had been foggy earlier and the moisture still lingered. Had I not already seen it, I would still know. I could smell it. This condition happens every June where we lived and I had never once paused long enough to really take it in. To let it fill me up. It was a sweet smell. Late spring. Flowers. Which ones, I wondered. I should take the time to be able to tell one from the other. Later. Shaggy was on the move.

He paused atop a big boulder looking out over his domain, taking it all in. I followed suit. *Wow*, I thought. It's really spectacular this time of day. The green valleys below, the distant mountains, the long shadows from the morning sun still low in the sky. We sat there for quite a long time, just looking, absorbing. A ground squirrel darted across the hill below us and I prayed that Shaggy wouldn't chase it. My knees weren't up to it.

Next, it was over to a grassy field we both know, and Shaggy embraced it like a kid at the circus for the first time. He bounced and leaped, and I followed him around, checking out every little thing. I even got down on my ancient knees and sniffed the grass. It smelled *good*. It really did. Have you ever gotten on your belly and sniffed. It reminded me of the freshly cut grass in our yard when I was a kid. And baseball. And Shaggy thought this was *fun!*

After a bit, he rolled over on his back and began to wriggle and scratch with the biggest smile on his face I've ever seen. I did the same. It felt *good*. There was a moment of hope that no one in the neighborhood would happen by and wonder if I had lost my mind. And I had to consciously dismiss the grass stains I was certain were accumulating on my clothes. But mostly I just wriggled and scratched and enjoyed it. And soaked up the warmth of the morning sun.

Next Shaggy flopped over on his side, sighed – yes, actually, audibly, *sighed* – and just lay there. After a bit his eyes drifted shut. Mine too.

It wasn't a long nap, but a good one. I know it had to be better for my health to start a day this way. I realized, of course, it wouldn't happen every day. But with Shaggy there to remind me, to be ever anxious to do it again, to be so deliriously excited about seemingly so little, it *would* happen every so often. And I would be better for it. I've read all the studies about how stress causes just about everything in your body to go wrong. And how eliminating stress, or lowering stress levels can turn things around. We all know it's true, but we rarely, seriously, do anything about it.

Dog knows best. Dog is *on it!* And he or she is always there to remind us. But we must pay attention for it to work. We must watch. Observe. And apply. Our family is fortunate to live out in the country. For me, it works better to be away from throngs of people. Some people prefer the throngs. But if you're locked in a city, you can always put Fido in the car and drive away to the country every once in a while. Just to watch. And learn. The concepts you pick up can be applied anywhere. Slow down. Enjoy the things around you, the things you breeze right past most of the time. Close your eyes and sniff. See colors, flowers. Stop and smell the roses. Take a short nap.

Have you ever noticed how many short naps your dog takes every day? And how they refresh him or her?

Give it a try. Watch your dog. Inside and out. Follow her lead. Don't worry about feeling foolish. Stop and allow the experience of fresh air and wind in your face to be pure ecstasy.

You will soon be looking at life quite differently.

"The reason a dog has so many friends is that he wags his tail instead of his tongue."

*Annonymous*

# 2

# JUST DO IT

Skilo here. Australian Terrier. I guess you could say I'm one of Joe and Kathleen's pack. And I've noticed something you need to consider.

It has taken years and years of your human research to discover what we of the tail-wagging brotherhood have known forever: whenever a new set of circumstances is presented to you, your initial reaction, your very first split-second thought on the subject is, almost always, the best response. The right answer. It has to do with a lot of deep psycho mumbo jumbo that none of us really need to understand. You can go read all the studies... or read the book *Blink*... or you can listen to me.

Or your own dog.

Don't second guess. Don't say *what if.* Don't start with the excuses. Listen to your first response. Do what you know is right. Every time. That's our mantra. *Just do it.*

Whenever my humans come rolling in two hours late and I'm having quite a good time, thank you, gnawing the leg off the new coffee table, do I stop and debate whether I want to stick with the fun? Do I pout and decide I will ignore them for being late? Nope. The first response is: *Go and greet my loved ones! Smother them with kisses! Tell them I love them and I'm tickled they are back home.* It makes them feel good, and makes me feel terrific.

And it's the right thing to do.

Love, you see, is unconditional.

By definition.

Why don't humans get that?

Seriously. I mean, how many times have you heard some two-legger say, "Dogs are just amazing. Their love is so unconditional." Love has always been unconditional until humans got their precious thumbs on it. But *conditional* love isn't love. It's something else.

*I'll get to it in a minute. I love you but I'm so busy. I'm upset because you forgot to put away the peanut butter. Your grades are slipping. Why isn't dinner ready?*

And here's my favorite: *I'm too stressed right now.*

That human can scratch one of us on the head, look into our eyes, talk sweetly about loving things… but can't do it with their own family. Do you have any idea how many of you are just like us, longing for a gentle touch, a hug, a quiet moment? *Just hold me. Show me that that I matter.*

Try this with your spouse, your daughter or son, your mom or dad. You'll feel just as good we do. And *they*'ll feel even better. Seriously. Try it. Love your humans like your dog.

You'll probably have to overcome the likelihood that the humans you are loving unconditionally will be just as wrapped up in extraneous conditions as you were a few moments ago. I've often wondered if the vertical human-to-dog relationship isn't affected by some sort of misplaced human guilt: *I feel sorry for a dumb animal that has no better sense than to love me no matter how poorly I treat it.* Whatever the reason, when it happens there's a displacement of all the conditions, a melting away of the negative energy, an exchange of love. And a result.

Everybody feels better. Is happier. But when it's human to human, there's a complexity layer that doesn't come up when it's human to dog. It *shouldn't* come up *ever*, but it does. And it doesn't need to. We canines know these things, and you can learn from us. Watch your dog.

We don't love our humans only if dinner is on time.

We don't love our humans only if their grades are good.

We don't love our humans only when they pay attention to us.

We don't love our humans only if they never scold us.

Shouldn't you love *your* humans the same way?

Love doesn't stop when someone hurts your feelings.

Love doesn't stop when someone doesn't share.

Love doesn't stop when you're being ignored.

Love doesn't stop when you don't get your way.

Love doesn't stop at all. Not real love.

It's unconditional.

Allow yourself to love unconditionally, and be loved. To touch and feel. To focus on what's really important, and to make all your choices from that base. Then watch what happens. I do. Most dogs do. What can you learn from that?

I wonder.

You should too.

"If you pick up a starving dog and make him prosperous, he will not bite you. This is the principal difference between a dog and a man."

*Mark Twain*

# 3

## ARE YOU LISTENING?

Do you listen to your dog?

*I have no choice in the matter. He barks incessantly at the cat next door?*

That's not exactly what I mean. Do you listen to what he's saying to you?

*Are you one of those whackos who claims to read an animal's thoughts?*

No. But dogs do talk you know.

*Really?*

The woman on the other side of this conversation was now beginning to step backward, looking for the door.

But the truth is dogs do speak to you. And in so doing they once again demonstrate our shortcomings. This discovery changed my life.

It all began many years ago when the family was watching a clip from *Lady and the Tramp* on a Sunday night Disney program as we finished dinner.

Tramp, a wiry, scoundrel of a mutt from the wrong side of the tracks comes to the rescue of the sheltered Lady, a bashful, beautiful, pedigreed spaniel from a proper home, and true love blooms. I've never forgotten the scene in the alley behind Tony's Italian Ristorante when Tony himself sings *Bella Notte* to Tramp and Lady as they unknowingly nibble up the same noodle from a plate of spaghetti and find themselves, blushingly, nose to nose.

I sat, totally entranced, gazing at the television set as if it were a living, breathing thing, feeling quite silly because I couldn't control the emotions welling within me. But something else was beginning to stir, like a baby chick pecking and poking its way out of an egg. And quite suddenly I found myself toying with a curious idea.

As we ferried the dinner plates into the kitchen, I asked Carolyn if she thought it would be possible to film a story as strong and emotionally involving as *Lady and the Tramp*, told completely from a dog's point-of-view... but with *real* dogs instead of animation.

She looked at me as if I were nuts. And that's where it all began.

We tossed it around as we loaded the dishwasher. Disney's dogs could talk and real dogs, of course, couldn't. Or *shouldn't*. That's the mysterious difference between animation and live-action. Animation somehow lifts us across the threshold into the animals' own world. When we hear them speak, it's not really English, as we know it. It's some sort of magical translation that allows us to eavesdrop and understand what they're saying without suspending our belief in them as real creatures. But if Lassie were to appear on the screen and start talking, believability would go right out the window. We would no longer accept her as a real dog, but rather as something manufactured by the movie people. Cute, sometimes, maybe good for a laugh, but *not* the stuff for creating romantic adventure as emotionally satisfying as *Lady and the Tramp.*

For this type of story to work, the audience must care a great deal for the central characters, and such emotional attachments evolve only when the story is told believably through the eyes and feelings of those characters; dogs in this case, *real* dogs who cannot talk. "But how in the world," I puzzled, "do you get the story across when your lead characters never utter a word?"

"A narrator might work," Carolyn said.

Gross. I reached deep into the diaphragm for a facsimile of James-Earl-Jones-mellow. *"And then Spot, thinking that Dick and Jane must surely be in perilous trouble, decided to risk the mighty leap from the top of the Sears Tower."*

That dealt me a dripping dishrag right to the face.

We continued to paint the idea into a corner. The very concept of a story from a dog's point-of-view meant that it could not be told through the eyes of people. Lassie stories, for example, were not really dog stories, but *human* stories, *about* a dog, from a *human's* point-of-view. Even animal stories without people, when told on film by a narrator, are unavoidably locked to the narrator's point-of-view. To create a story as wonderful, and as centered within a dogs' world as *Lady and the Tramp*, with real dogs, and with no acceptable way for them to communicate to an audience, I finally decided, was probably impossible.

As Carolyn went off to bed, dogs were still scratching around in my head. Even if the communication barrier could be breached, there was still the problem of story. Could a well-structured story be written, purely from a dog's point-of-view, that didn't violate a dog's ability to understand and react? Not allowed: the old scam where clever Rover appears out of nowhere and grabs clever guy by the pants leg causing clever guy to instantly shriek, "Great balls of fire! Rover wants us to follow him!"

I sat for the better part of an hour trying to read, but I was really watching our little dog prowl around the room. A lab barking next door got his attention. Then a siren down the street. I watched his playful tracking of a moth flitting across the carpet, and studied his responses to my changing moods. I dropped to the floor and started barking. The puzzled look on his face spoke volumes, and made me laugh out loud. I rolled around, scratched the carpet, and even huddled in the corner and shivered as if I was deathly afraid of him. His concern for his master's sanity was as clear as if he had spoken it.

I had never really *listened* to him before. Had never realized how much dogs *speak* with their eyes and moods and attitudes. By the time I turned out the lights, I was no longer certain that it couldn't be done. Dogs, I was discovering, do talk, quite loudly in fact, with their faces, their bodies, their ears, and especially their eyes. Like a human, a dog will radiate with happiness, or wilt like a flower in sadness. When angry, the sparks are unmistakable; when afraid, the fear indisputable. Anxious, they'll flit about nervously, tightly strung, eyes darting from one thing to another. Content, they'll settle like a reflective sigh, relaxed and calm, with the mood reading like an open book. Pay attention and you will always know what they're feeling, thinking, caring about. What they're going to do next. And what they're *not*.

Or so it was with Sir Benjamin of Courtney, our little Yorkshire Terrier. He had never really known his registered name, of course. He answered, simply, to Benji.

The next morning I arose at 4:00 am and wrote the entire *Benji* story before heading off to my *real* job at an advertising agency. The rest, as they say, is history. Five Benji movies all of which rely solely on the eyes of the dog for dialog.

I never stopped peering into the eyes of the three dogs who starred in those five movies, always trying to understand what they were thinking, or saying. And how I might cajole them to think or say what the script called for. The same is true with the myriad other dogs we've had through the years. I *listened* to their eyes, trying to pay as much attention to their feelings and emotions and desires as they did to mine. Trying to *hear* what they were saying to me. But I cannot explain why it took years for me to realize that I should be doing the same in the world of humans.

How often I've caught myself in mid-conversation not listening at all to what the other party was saying, so tangled up in what I would be saying next that I was hearing none of the other side. In other words, it was all about me.

And that, of course, is the wrong answer. For conversation, relationship, or life.

My dogs taught me that.

I often wonder why they had to.

The goal in life is to be as good a person as
your dog already thinks you are.

*Anonymous*

# 4

## NEVER LOOK BACK

We had a Yorkshire Terrier whose name was Chelsea. In the last few years of her life I began to think she must have cat genes buried in her soul because I swear she had nine lives. It seems like everything that *could* happen to her, *did* happen to her. We were taking the trash cans down to the road in our gator (a motorized golf-cart-like vehicle we use around the farm for various chores) and Chelsea was riding along in the back... until she spotted a squirrel. Now, realize, at the time she was approaching fifteen. But without a thought, she leaped out of the back of the gator, landed funny on her left hind leg, and popped it out of the socket, taking the cartilage along with it. The surgery to put it back in the socket and wire it in place was long (and expensive) and her recuperation took seemingly forever. But the smile never left her face.

Not long after that, I fell off a ladder while working on the roof of a small shed. Fortunately nothing was broken and there was no surgery, but the rib pain was pretty intense for a few weeks... and a smile was the furthest thing from my mind. I moaned and groaned and bitched like a banshee. I blatantly begged for sympathy, and was crabby for weeks because I had been so stupid to not tie off the ladder.

Now the medically proven reality, the reality that Chelsea innately understood and acted on, is that a happy inner self heals better and faster than a crabby, whining, bitchy self. It's true. As I said, it's medically proven. The inner chemistry, hormones and stuff, released by a happy, smiling self work to heal... and that same stuff is depleted, reduced, suppressed when you allow yourself to be sad, depressed, or angry. Moreover, all that time I spent moaning or griping was time completely wasted. It accomplished nothing. Nada! I would have been much better to follow Chelsea's example and stop fretting about things in the past. Put a smile on my face and move on. Think of someone *other* than myself.

Every dog we've ever loved has been that way. No matter how bad things got, they were thinking only of us. It's that unconditional love thing again.

What is it about we humans that beg for sympathy and brood so over the least little accident or error in judgment? It's in the past. Nothing can be done about it. It happened. It cannot be reclaimed or changed.

A realtor friend was telling me about a client who had rejected an offer of $890,000 for his house less than two months before. He had countered at $900,000, and the buyer walked away. In the two months that followed, the market dropped and he was now having to consider an offer of $778,000. More than a $100,000 loss in two months. Frustrating, yes. But my realtor friend said the client was in a near depression about it.

And there's nothing in the world that could be done to change it. What's done is done. Worry, fretting, sadness about the drop will help nothing. Do as your dog would do. Forget it. Make a new decision, and move on.

Difficult?

Yes.

Impossible?

No.

The last Benji movie, *Benji Off the Leash,* was not a big success like those that had gone before. It was unable to compete as an independent film against the huge promotional dollars being spent by the Hollywood studios these days. That experience left a huge, gaping hole in my life. I was convinced that *Benji Off the Leash* was going to raise the bar for family films. Be an example that would show Hollywood the error of its ways. It had a strong story that set a good example, without the use of four-letter words, sexual innuendos, or violence. I was certain that God was using *Benji Off the Leash* to prove once and for all that good stories do not need to lower the bar to entertain. But the film did not do well.

And there was this huge hole to fill.

When depression tries to claw its ugly self into your being, there are but two choices. Give in to it, or grab it by its scrawny neck, sling it to the ground, and pull yourself out of that hole.

Do what Chelsea would do. Don't look back. Focus on another need. Another place to make a difference.

When I quit moaning and groaning and looking backward, when I finally turned my eyes and thoughts to *what next*, suddenly a new passion arose, and with it a new career. A journey of discovery and a revelation that something was amiss with the traditional methods of teaching and caring for... horses. Which gave birth to *The Soul of a Horse*, a book published by the largest publisher in the country. A book that is changing the way thousands and thousands of people think about horses, and about themselves. A book that has become a national best seller and is in its eleventh printing.

Thanks, at least in part, to Chelsea.

Dog knows best. Dog is *on it!* At least ours are. And I suspect yours are too.

In his book *Marley and Me*, John Grogan tells us the lesson our dogs teach us, "The secret to a good life: Never slow down. Never look back. Live each day with adolescent verve and spunk and curiosity and playfulness."

You'll be healthier.

And definitely happier.

I like dogs because they never pretend
to be something they're not.

*Anonymous*

# 5

## IF YOU WANT WHAT LIES BURIED, DIG UNTIL YOU FIND IT

Have you ever seen a dog give up?

Have you ever even heard of a dog giving up?

When Benji sees a gopher hole, our entire property is in danger.

What do you suspect she's thinking?

*Awww, man. That hole's way too small, I'll never get in there. And the dirt is so hard. Maybe I'll hang out until it rains. Soften things up. Yeah, that's what I'll do. Besides, since the hole is so small, it's probably just a baby gopher. Too small to mess with. Yeah, way too small. Waste of time. If I only had a shovel. Or maybe I could get someone else to dig it for me. If someone would just bring me a gopher, that'd be cool. No digging at all. Yeah, that's it. I'll just wait until someone brings me a gopher.*

How familiar does that sound?

And how shameful?

Dogs don't work that way. They don't give up. Ever. Whether it's the story of the lost dog who crossed three states to get back home to his master, or the dogs who are now being written up in medical journals for saving their masters from cancer, or predicting seizures, or doing for the disabled what the disabled cannot do for themselves, there is simply no such thing as giving up.

Doesn't happen.

When Benji sees that gopher hole, if I don't happen to be around to divert her and fill in the hole, it'll look like Grand Canyon by tomorrow. And the funny thing is, she doesn't want to hurt the gopher. *I* might, but she doesn't. She wants to protect it. Mommy it. It's her way. And she would dig into next week to get to it.

Persistence. That's how you get things done.

Don't ever give up.

Dogs know that.

That's why all the Benji movies have been about persistence. Not quitting in the face of seemingly insurmountable odds. At the core of the original Benji movie was a dog who refused to give up when he couldn't find a way to communicate an important piece of information to humans who needed to know. Every struggle that ended in failure brought more persistence. Greater effort.

In a way, that's also the essence of how you, and the rest of the world, came to know that first movie. When the story was initially written, it was rejected by all of Hollywood. When, finally, we raised enough money independently to produce the film, it was, again, rejected by all of Hollywood for distribution.

This was not the result we had worked so long and hard for, overcoming obstacle after obstacle, raising money, producing the picture, putting an all-new concept on the screen: a dog actually acting, expressing emotion, involving the audience in his struggle.

After editing, we had to stop everything, raise still more money and write three new sequences because the movie was too short to be a theatrical feature. That's when I was ready to give up. But I didn't, and when the film was finally finished audiences loved it. The emotion was working. For the first time in history, a dog was acting on the screen.

But the distributors didn't get it. They all turned it down.

We had two choices: throw it in the trash, or figure it out. We chose the latter.

Which meant raising even more money, forming a distribution company, about which we knew nothing, doing a lot more learning, and releasing the film ourselves. I had studied advertising and marketing and been with a couple of advertising agencies, so I was confident we could do it. But our first marketing efforts were mediocre at best. I was dead wrong in the way I had evaluated the market. We had to change the entire program three times before we got it right. But after almost three-and-a-half years of effort, with doors slamming in our faces every step of the way, we eventually did get it right. And, according to Variety, *Benji* was the number three picture of the year.

Persistence.

Don't ever give up.

My friend Andy Andrews tells the story about the Aborigine tribes in Australia who are known for their rain making talents. Planters call on these tribes whenever there isn't enough rain. Some tribes are more successful than others, but one year word began to spread around about a particular tribe who never failed. They were always successful. A big planter decided to track down this tribe, which he did, and he was granted an audience with the king.

"I've heard that you never fail to make rain," the planter told the king. "Is that true?"

"Absolutely true," the king replied.

"How do you do that?" the planter asked. "How is it possible to be successful one hundred percent of the time?"

The king looked at him for a long moment, and smiled.

"We don't quit until it rains."

I love that story because the king's approach guarantees success. You can never fail... until you quit. If you are committed to never giving up, to being ever persistent, to not quitting *until it rains*, you will always be successful.

Dogs know this.

What would the world be like if more of us did?

"Don't accept your dog's admiration as conclusive evidence that you are wonderful."

*Ann Landers*

# 6

## WHEELS DO TURN

Thin, delicate eyebrows arched skeptically over rolling eyes and the lady smiled sweetly. "I can't print that, Mr. Camp. Tell me about the story, and the actors."

She was giving me a clue, handwriting on the wall -- or in this case in the Dallas Morning News -- but I wasn't listening. I was too astonished. I had just spent thirty minutes ranting giddily about the unique concept of a dog *acting,* about the incredible facial expressions Benji was giving us, about those big brown eyes and the reams of dialog they were speaking, about the dog himself and how for the first time I had come to realize that the story we were telling wasn't purely the emotional petition I had once thought but, in reality, quite plausible. Dogs, I had discovered, *can* think rationally. And this particular one was extraordinary.

Not that others aren't. But most dogs who have the intelligence, attitude and temperament to do what Benji was doing, never have the opportunity to learn and to gain the vocabulary that the various Benji's have had.

"Vocabulary?! That's ridiculous!"

I bit my tongue because we were on the air. A radio talk show in Norfolk, Virginia. I was promoting the original Benji movie. The host went on to imply that I was as full of dark brown bull droppings as any Hollywood hype artist.

But Norfolk radio notwithstanding, dogs can develop a vocabulary. And understand concepts. Like the concept of *other*. If you ask Benji for a foot, then ask for the *other* foot, he switches. If he walks off and the trainer tells him to go the *other* way, he looks back to see *which* other way, then takes the point and heads in that direction. He understands the concept of words like *slow, hurry, easy,* and *not,* no matter how the words are applied. When asked to perform a difficult task, you can actually witness the process as he studies the situation to determine the best approach. But none of this is particularly unusual. Sheep dogs in Europe tend entire flocks *by themselves* for months, keeping the sheep together, deciding when to move them from one pasture to another, even stopping the whole group to check for vehicles before crossing a road.

At a press conference in a Miami hotel suite, a dozen reporters watched the first Benji perform one of his standard show routines, completely unaware -- until they were told later -- that he had made a mess of it and would've never finished had he not been able to think it through.

He was wedged between two banister poles, pulling a coffee mug tied to a string of leashes up to the mezzanine level which overlooked the group below. A person, of course, would use two hands, one over the other, but Benji used his mouth and a foot. He reached down and pulled up a length, held it tightly against the floor with his foot, then reached down again and pulled up another length, held it with his foot, and so on, until he had retrieved whatever was tied to the other end. As he performed, the leash slipped over the corner of the mezzanine floor and, because he was so snugly wedged between the banister poles, he could no longer reach it with the foot he had always used to hold it. I marveled as I watched the wheels turn. He pondered the situation for only a few seconds before he, quite logically, placed the *other* foot on the rope -- the foot he had *never* before used to hold it -- and went on with the routine as if nothing had happened.

Benji even understands what he's doing when he's acting.

*"Now you've heard it all folks. The dog understands he's acting! I suppose he gets script approval!"*

Chicago. Another talk show host.

One of the more important sequences in that first movie involved Benji moping forlornly, aimlessly through town. He knew the children were in danger but was unable to communicate what he knew to the family, who had, in fact, scolded him for trying. For the sequence to work, indeed for the entire *story* to work, these scenes had to generate unencumbered empathy and support for Benji's plight. He had to look as if he had lost his last friend. His desperation had to reach out from those big brown eyes and squeeze passionately upon the hearts of the audience.

It worked so well, that during the first rehearsal, I almost aborted the sequence. I was forty feet above the scene with our cameraman in the bucket of a cherry picker -- the kind utility companies use to fix power lines -- and Frank Inn, Benji's trainer and clearly one of the best who ever lived, was in the alley below *screaming* at the star, "*Shame on you!! Put your head down!! Shame, shame on you!!*"

Benji looked as if he had, *in fact*, lost his last friend. It was perfect. I *believed* him. But I couldn't bear to see him hurt so from the scolding.

I asked the grip controlling the cherry picker to lower me back to the ground and I walked into the scene and asked Frank to hold for a minute while we talked.

"What's the matter?" he asked, eyes wide and curious. "Isn't this the look you want?"

"It's perfect," I said. "But I don't feel right about getting it this way."

"What the hell are you talking about?"

"I don't feel right about you scolding Benji like that."

Frank's eyes rolled heavenward. "Turn around," he said. "Does that look like a scolded dog?"

Benji was aimlessly scratching his ear. He looked up at me and yawned idly.

"Watch closely," said Frank. He motioned Benji onto his feet and began scolding him again. Our floppy-eared star's head dropped like a rock, his eyes drooped and he looked as pitiful as anything I had ever seen. Then Frank relaxed, chirped a simple "Okay," and as if he had flipped an emotional switch, Benji blinked away the blues, had a good shake, wagged his tail, and awaited Frank's next command. He fully understood what was going on, and scolding wasn't it. He might not have known the word, but he was, in the truest sense, acting. Perhaps when Frank began training this routine, the first time Benji was scolded, he might have thought he had done something wrong. But the minute he was rewarded for the sad look and praised heartily, he very quickly came to understand. Dogs are very intuitive, so be careful what you say and do around them. You might be teaching them something you'd rather not.

Benji picked things up so quickly that he even astonished Frank on occasion. Like the time we realized he had deciphered what *cut* and *print* meant. Frank unraveled from beneath a pile of people on the floor by the camera and suddenly realized his dog was nowhere in sight. "Your dog's no fool," a grip chuckled. "Joe said 'cut' and he split for the air conditioning."

Attached to our portable air conditioner was a fifty-foot hose, fifteen inches in diameter, and attached to the end of that was a little cubicle enclosed on the top and bottom and two sides. This was Benji's home between shots. The air was necessary to keep him from panting.

He learned very quickly that the air conditioner was *his* and that's where he was supposed to be when the camera wasn't rolling. It didn't take him long to figure out that the camera quit rolling whenever I said "Cut." So off he'd go, without a word from Frank. Whenever I said "Print," the shot was probably over, another one checked off the list, and Benji would prance happily over to Frank's wife, Juanita, and gather up a few "Good boys."

The current Benji is just as intuitive. Our bedroom is upstairs and there's one particular door at the top of the stairs that, if left open, becomes a funnel for heat as it rises through the house. Benji knows how to open that door to go in, but she never shuts it. One day I decided: okay, enough. If you're going to open it, you're going to have to shut it as well. I laid in wait for her to come up the stairs and push the door open with her foot.

"Uhh, uhh, uhh," I said to her. "Get back over there and shut the door."

It took maybe ten minutes, with all she already knew, to teach her to close that door with her foot. Now, *if* I'm in the room when she comes in, she'll close it straightaway, without me even asking her to. *If* I'm in the room.

I have spied on her and watched her ease through the door, scan the room to see if I was around, glance back at the door, and make the choice not to close it.

Makes me laugh.

She's been living around people too long.

There's a side benefit, by the way, to using real vocabulary to teach. The words can, and will, apply to other things. Benji now knows what *open* and *shut* mean, and those words can be applied to *any* door, or cabinet, or box, or book. But beware. That knowledge has forced us to rearrange the cabinets in the kitchen to keep all food out of reach.

Your dog, like Benji, can think rationally. Can figure things out. Can make decisions about when to do something and when not to.

And yet he still loves you.

Unconditionally.

Can't we learn to do that?

"A dog is the only thing on earth that loves you more than he loves himself."

*– Josh Billings*

# 7

# LEAD, FOLLOW, OR GET OUT OF THE WAY

Josie here. Joe and Kathleen's Australian Shepherd. The cutest one of the bunch.

Have you ever noticed that dogs have no trouble at all choosing their leaders... or following them? That's because the leader *is* a leader. Proven. Assured. Comfortable in the role because she knows she can do it. (Okay, I suppose it *could* be a *he*.) And the pack follows willingly because they know they're in good hands. They trust and respect their leader because the leader has earned that trust and respect. They know he will be responsible for the pack *before* himself. Decisions will be made for the good of the pack.

Sound like a good model?

Amongst the pack, there's never – or at least rarely – a question. There are no second-guessers. You prove your leadership capability, and the followers *follow*. No arguments. *You're the man, er, dog. Lead until you bust your pick, and we'll follow you anywhere.* And we all know that being a good follower is just as important as being a good leader. It's called teamwork.

You humans could learn from that.

The same relationship works between you and your dog. If you ever want to know whether or not you are the leader, whether or not you have achieved the status of *alpha* with your dog(s), try this experiment. Go open the door, with your dog at your heels. Don't open it all the way, maybe just a couple of feet. Then, just stand there. If the dog waits for you to go out first, or at least looks to you for an okay, before darting out the door, then you are to be congratulated. In your dog's mind, you are the leader. You will go first, to see if it's safe, or you will at least acknowledge that it's safe before he goes. You are to be trusted. You are to be listened to. If the dog just goes for it, racing out the door to attack whatever varmint that might be invading your yard at the moment, then he considers himself the leader. Or perhaps he just considers himself leader*less*.

Your relationship will improve if you fix that.

Here's the thing. If you choose to be leader, whether with your dog or other humans, then invest the time and energy to be a good leader. A trusted leader. A respected leader. An effective leader. Always remembering that if you lead wisely, you'll be followed cheerfully. If you can't (or won't) do that, then be content to follow. But be a good follower.

Have you ever seen one of us sit back and snipe at our leader? *Oh I don't want to do that. This would be better. I could do your job better than you.* If that's the case, then *do* it! Otherwise, shut up and get on the team. The opposite of teamwork is anarchy, and it simply doesn't work. A society, a group, a pack cannot function with all chiefs. Things implode. Fall apart. Folks bicker, usually about stuff that's not worth the effort. We of the fluffy set don't do it that way. We know better. Apply the mantra at the head of this chapter to your club, your church, your town, the world and see how much better things work. Trust me on this. Dog knows best.

"My hunch is that people who act more like dogs have happier marriages. That's assuming, of course, you don't marry someone who emulates cats."

*John Grogan*

# 8

## EVERY RULE HAS ITS EXCEPTIONS

Wow! You live with Benji??

I hear it all the time.

*What's it like?*

*Is she a spoiled starlet? Is she a diva?*

*Does she ever get to do doggie things?*

Does she ever!

Turn your back for a moment and she's up to her cute floppy earlobes in DIRT, digging after some gopher or ground squirrel. It's even better yet if it's been raining. The DIRT is MUD, which is softer. And this always happens the day before we have to leave on a plane to make an appearance somewhere! When we lived in California she loved to hide in the bushes and follow a car or truck or the UPS van through the gate... *outside* the gate, where coyotes lived and hunted by the hundreds. And huge hawks and eagles and owls. And at least one cougar we'd seen. Not to mention traffic.

Her coat, unlike our other four dogs, is very fine ("*Oh, she's so-o-o-o-o soft!*") which picks up and clings like glue to every cocklebur, twig, sticker, and weed that exists. Oh, and her diet?? Would you believe avocados and horse poop!! Never mind how gross (Hmmm, this guacamole tastes a bit different). Try to keep her figure down to movie weight with that diet everywhere she turns... anytime of day... for free.

*Is she really as smart as she appears in the movies?*

Well, except for the questionable activities above I have to say *yes*.

Too much so for her own good, much less ours. She can pretty much get out of any confinement into which she might be placed to keep her out of the mud, away from the cockleburs, away from the gate to the world outside, away from the manure and the avocados! All, while the other three dogs merely watch in amazement and puzzlement (*How DOES she do that?).*

She *is* her own dog. All the while being as loyal a dog as I have ever seen. When I'm at home, she virtually never leaves my side. She's under my desk, at my feet, as I type this. If I get up and go up to the bedroom, she follows. Always there. I suspect because I'm the one who took her out of the shelter down in Mississippi.

Shortly after we adopted her, we were in New York to introduce the new Benji to the nation on ABC's *Good Morning America.* The first thing we always do when we're going to New York is make dinner reservations. There's no place like New York for great food. When we arrived, ABC had placed an especially nice dog crate in the room so we could go out for dinner. We had no way of knowing that Benji was going to have none of it. She had been abandoned once, thank you very much, and if she had anything to do with it, it was not going to happen again. When we left the room, she exploded. Yelping, barking, raising a proper ruckus.

We immediately scurried back in, expecting hotel security at any moment. Benji was very pleased with herself. We let her out of the crate, put a used t-shirt on the bed for her to cuddle, even turned on the television. When we left again, she almost tore the door down.

Frustrated, we phoned one very, very nice restaurant, cancelled our reservation, and ordered room service. As we ate that night, with Benji stretched out on the bed happy as a clam, Kathleen and I pondered aloud what could have possibly happened in her past to cause such worry about being left alone. Those conversations became the foundation for the fifth Benji movie (this dog's first), *Benji Off the Leash.*

At home, she's fine when we leave. There are four other dogs, and she knows she's at home. But I've never left her alone in a hotel room since that day in New York, which puts certain limitations on a whole host of activities.

"You know, that can be fixed," a vet once told me.

"Why?" I responded.

"It's not good to have a dog so fixated on you," she said.

"Why?" I asked again.

"Because you are being coerced into doing the dog's will."

"It's not about me," I said.

The vet blinked. Twice. And changed the subject.

Benji's unconditional love is not about her so why should mine be conditional and about me? *I love you when you're easy. When you don't cause a problem. When you overcome your very rational fears and sit quietly while we're gone.* That's what this dog has taught me. Benji and all of the other dogs we have and have had in the past. I keep telling myself if I were more like them everyday, with everyone I know, I'd be a much better human.

I try. Sometimes. But my nature wins too often. Yet she is always there to remind me and that makes me smile. And try harder.

During the filming of her first movie, Benji was living with her trainer, Genny Kerns. Genny had tried to tell me that I should stay completely away from her on the set because she was so bonded to me that it would be difficult for Genny to keep her attention. I knew right away that wouldn't work. How does the director stay away from his star? And, I felt Genny wasn't giving this very bright and intuitive dog enough credit.

"Let's try it this way, " I finally said. "Every morning, when you arrive on the set, let Benji find me, say good morning, and get a good hug. Then I think she'll be fine."

And she was.

We have three dogs from shelters and two from breeders and I'm convinced there's a different bond with dogs rescued from a shelter. I believe they know they've been in a potentially bad circumstance and they draw closer immediately. We love all four dogs. But

Benji and Shaggy are different. The bond is stronger. Benji with me. Shaggy and Sadie with Kathleen.

When Kathleen goes downstairs in the morning, before taking the kids to school, all the dogs go out... except Benji. She's still upstairs waiting for me to wade through shaving, exercise, vitamins, the ritual. She's not anxious. Not in a hurry. Just waiting. Patiently. Finally, when she sees I'm done, when the boots go on, she gets excited and dances around ready to begin her day. She follows me down the stairs and goes straight out the door. Off to the things that make her happy.

Like the mud, and the horse poop.

Are these really exceptions to the rule that dog knows best?

I don't think so. Not really. Someone once said: *Do what you like, and like what you do.* Benji does exactly that. And I'll bet your dog does as well.

And so should we.

"Properly trained a man can be dog's best friend."

*Corey Ford*

# 9

## FIDO IN THE BOARDROOM

I had a friend once who always took his dog to work with him. A *big* fluffy Malamute, so he wasn't easy to hide. The friend was president of a small successful company, and throughout the day, the dog would lie at his feet, follow him around the office, and accompany him to sales pitches, meetings, and negotiations.

"Don't folks ever get a little weird when you walk in with a dog," I asked him once. "Especially one who looks like a wolf!" Which this one did, but he was one of the sweetest, kindest dogs I ever met.

"Take me, take my dog, I tell them," the friend said.

"Why complicate your life that way," I wondered aloud. "Does your dog really miss you that much?"

"Oh, it's not for Shotsy," he said. "It's for me. I am definitely a better person when Shotsy is around."

"Huh?"

He's not serious, I thought. I've lived with dogs all my life, and loved them all, but this was a new concept.

"Oh yeah," my friend said. "If ever, for example, I'm about to shade the truth in a meeting to make things appear more, shall we say, valuable… well, I look down at Shotsy, and he looks at me, as if to say, *I wouldn't do that. Why would you?* And I don't."

"The dog is your conscience?"

"You could say that I suppose. But it's more about seeing this incredible hulk, right there before me, caring more for me than anything else in the world, without even a smidgen of dishonesty or cruelness or selfishness in his bones."

"We need more dogs in congress," I said.

Years later I thought about my old friend and his malamute after we had adopted the third Benji from a shelter in Mississippi and we began to travel around the country together promoting her first movie and doing fund-raisers and benefits for animal shelters and rescue organizations. And I began to pay attention to me, and how different I seemed to be when out on the road with this dog. I felt myself being nicer, softer, not so (pardon) dogmatic. I would catch myself looking at her (yes, number three is a female) whenever a story-stretch was creeping into mind, like rounding *up* the figures relating to her movie. She would look at me with those big brown eyes and I couldn't help but take a step backward and remind myself that twisting a truth would never enter her mind. And that's about as right as anything could be. Perhaps it's not accidental that *dog* spelled backward is *God*.

Shortly thereafter Benji began to go lots of places with me, not just promotional or appearance travel. We'd go shopping, to horse shows, to visit friends, and, yes, even to business meetings. And I was better for it.

Unfortunately, we're all human. And God gave us a free will with which to corrupt ourselves... or not. But it's clearly not easy, the *not* part. There are so many chances everyday to make poor choices. To affect someone else negatively. To be selfish, or downright mean. But with a dog in our lap, there is a constant and emotional reminder of selfless, unconditional love. Of choosing right over wrong. Good over bad. In short, of being more dog-like. And, even though some folks might think it nuts, I've discovered there is simply nothing in the world wrong with that.

"If you think dogs can't count, try putting three dog biscuits in your pocket and then giving Fido only two of them."

*Phil Pastoret*

# 10

## THEY DO KNOW BEST

I gazed down into Chelsea's eyes as we waited for the vet. She was wrapped in a fluffy towel in Kathleen's arms. I couldn't mistake how comfortable she looked, how happy. But I was squeezing back tears, attempting to keep the promise I had made. She was sixteen now. We had been here when she was fifteen, but a miracle drug had given her another year. As I scratched her head and searched those wistful eyes, I found myself thinking about the question I had asked her so many times. A question I know she would've answered, if only she could. It had been the worst day of my life, and Chelsea was the only one left who knew exactly what happened. She had been there.

The doorbell rang again, and again, but there was no answer. The lady knocked loudly. It was all very curious. The luncheon had been set for a week.

More than curious, actually. There were no dogs barking. The dogs always barked and came running when she rang the doorbell.

She tried again.

Nothing.

Could she have written it down wrong?

She decided to return to her house, only a few blocks away, just to be certain. But her calendar confirmed the date and time. She tried calling her friend on the phone.

No answer.

Something was wrong. Something was very strange.

She returned to her friend's house and, again, rang the bell, and knocked. This time the dogs came immediately. Barking and yelping. Even more frantic than usual. Or so it seemed to her. But she kept telling herself she was over-reacting.

She tried the front door. It was locked.

She hurried around to the back, and tried the door to the screen porch. It was open, but the door to the house was locked. The dogs had followed her around and were barking even louder now, more frantic. The black one was practically climbing the curtains like a cat.

The lady tried a window, but it, too, was locked. The next one as well. But the next one wasn't.

She crawled through into the family room, and the dogs raced off toward the master bedroom. She followed, all the way into the master bath... where she found her friend collapsed on the tile floor.

A short time later the EMT's pronounced her friend dead of sudden cardiac arrest.

Her friend was Carolyn, my wife of thirty-eight years.

I was three thousand miles away about to climb on a plane, when I called home to check in, and my life shattered into pieces all over the airport floor. It was the longest plane ride anyone could ever take.

Chelsea was Carolyn's dog. Sassy was mine. She followed me everywhere. Always. But it was Chelsea's behavior that stuck in my brain, and my heart, as I muddled through a very dense fog for a very long time. Both dogs had been in the house when it happened. Both had clearly been with Carolyn when her friend was ringing the doorbell and banging on the door.

I've read that animals who are able to spend time with close companions who die, to digest the reality, be they of the same species or not, deal with it much better than those who don't have that special time. They seem to understand that death is part of life. Do they grieve, as such? Experts seem to agree that they do, for a short time. They miss the being they have been so close to and there is a hole where that existence lived. But given the opportunity to see the companion, to understand what has happened, their genetics lead on.

Chelsea proved the truth of that analysis, and much more. Chelsea proved to me, yet again, that we humans could learn so much from our dogs.

When Carolyn's friend was banging on our door, I believe Chelsea and Sassy were saying their goodbyes, letting it all sink in.

When I was picked up at the Raleigh airport, much later that night, I was barely lucid, but I remember being told that Chelsea had been very quiet, not her usual sprightly self. She had spent most of the evening lying on Carolyn's side of our bed.

When friends and family finally forced me into bed, both Chelsea and Sassy were there, right next to me, but Chelsea seemed especially to go the extra mile, to force me to rub her head. To crawl close and lick my face. I actually thought for a short period I was attending to her needs. But within a day, she had digested it all and was back chasing squirrels in the yard, guarding the house, barking at the mailman... and snuggling closer and more often with me than she ever had before. She had no more time for sadness. She had someone she needed to take care of. Another loved one to focus on. Someone who needed her. It would be wasteful to spend any more time in the past when there was someone in the here and now who needed her.

It took me almost a year to realize how right she was, how different life could be if we could see death of a loved one a bit more like Chelsea saw it. I don't mean leap into a frolic. We all need time to grieve. But I was pretty much in a depression for a year. I came as close to understanding why some people consider suicide as I ever want to come. There were people all over the place that could've used my help, my compassion, my understanding, but somehow I had let myself be consumed by selfish depression. Do you think Carolyn would've wanted that?

Had I only learned from Chelsea while it was happening. She had her time with Carolyn. She had her sadness. And, next, there was work to be done. People to heal. Had it not been for her, there's no telling how deep I might've gone. She seemed to always be there, to the point of getting in the way, whenever a wave of despair would roll over me. It certainly wasn't at the time, but looking back, it's almost humorous what a pest she became at just the right moment.

Eight years later, as she looked up at me from the towel in Kathleen's arms, I had promised her that I wouldn't give in to it again, no matter how much it might hurt. Tears were streaming down Kathleen's face, but I was holding on. I hugged Chelsea, and kissed her, and my finger reached out, as it had hundreds of time in the past, and touched the little tip of tongue that so often poked out between her front teeth. Touched it for the last time. And she smiled. And the vet came in.

Minutes later, I was in the car, having a good cry. A long one. A wet one. And then I did as I had promised Chelsea. I chose not to be selfish. I chose to focus on helping someone who needed me. For you see my new wife, Kathleen, had in a few short years, grown as close to Chelsea as Carolyn had been. I wiped away the wet, most of it, and said to her, "Let me tell you a story about Chelsea. It'll make you feel better. I promise."

Today, the tears still try to have their way when I think about her and all she did for me. In fact, as I write this, it's difficult to see the computer screen through the blur, but the tears are not just selfish tears.

They're tears of renewal, because with them always comes the promise to focus, not on myself, but on someone who needs me.

And so I do.

Dogs do know best.

"Avoid biting when a simple growl will do."

*Annonymous*

# 11

## UGLY

"That's the ugliest dog I've ever seen."

It was a guy. So I suppose we should forgive him. Men aren't known for being sensitive. Or deep.

"Dogs are cute. How can one possibly be that ugly."

This was a lady! Women are supposed to be able to see the inner beauty, right? The inner self. The worth.

All that.

But she was serious.

They were talking about Sadie.

A couple of months before Sadie was rescued from a shelter by Kathleen. We had moved from southern California to middle Tennessee.

At least one of us had. I had taken up residence in our new home in Tennessee and Kathleen would be staying in California until the twins had graduated from high school. They were both terrific students leading exemplary lives and we felt it would not be in their best interest to be uprooted in their junior year and moved across the country. So Kathleen and I would be living alone without each other for almost two years except for the weekend visits every few weeks.. I say alone but for me that was not completely accurate. I had the six horses, four dogs, and a cat.

Kathleen had the twins. Or so she thought.

Very quickly she came to understand that the last two years of high school could be very busy for a pair of teenagers involved in school organizations, high school musicals, dance programs, sports, and working as well.

Very busy indeed.

And thus it was very lonely around the empty rental house in California.

"I wish I had kept one of the dogs out here," she said during one of our nightly Skype sessions. "I'm just rattling around this empty house. It's lonely. And that makes me miss you more. I don't know what to do with myself."

"No luck finding a part time position?"

Kathleen's a lawyer who had been on her own handling a huge case for five years and when it was finally over we agreed that it had taken too much time away from the kids so she should take it easy for the last two years of their high school so she'd be available when needed. In touch and in tune, so to speak. And that was all fine before I, the dogs, the cat, and the horses left for Tennessee. I don't think she had ever been in such a state before.

"The only positions available in all of San Diego county are in collections and repossessions. I refuse to do that. There was one firm looking for a patent attorney but I know nothing about that field."

This was right in the middle of the 2009-2010 recession when everyone was cutting back not adding. And it was doubtful any decent position, even part time, would be open to someone who was known to be moving in less than two years. It was a conundrum. So without saying a word to me, or anyone for that matter, she made a clandestine trip down the hill into Escondido.

"Everybody says she's too ugly."

It was a young lady behind the counter at the local Humane Society.

"Not to me," Kathleen said. "I think she's cute."

The young lady shrugged and mumbled something about the eye of the beholder. Not what I would expect to hear from someone in the business of saving lives.

Like most of our horses and dogs, Sadie had chosen Kathleen. And that was that. With no serious thought to the fact that we already had four dogs. And a cat. Which I was taking care of alone over in Tennessee so I was, shall we say, experiencing every aspect of having multiple dogs.

The next thing I knew there was this weird looking fuzz ball jumping right into the middle of our Skype session that night.

"What the heck is that?" I exclaimed.

"That's Sadie. I rescued her today."

"Well..." I said, trying to think this thing through before inserting foot into mouth. "Yes, well... so... there she is. She's... uhh..."

"Don't you dare say she's ugly," Kathleen snapped.

Sadie weighed in at maybe six pounds. Skin and bones. Undernourished. But even at her optimum weight she probably wouldn't be an ounce over eight pounds. She was some kind of Chihuahua mix with thin wiry hair maybe three inches long that looked for the world like she had stuck a toe in an electrical outlet.

That's it. She looked like one of those Tom and Jerry cartoons.

And by comparison to all our other dogs she was tiny with a capital "T".

But she loved Kathleen. Had taken to her in one day like she had been with her all of her life.

They know.

Any dog who's been rescued knows. The bond between Benji and me is more potent than any I've ever experienced because I'm the one who took her away from that shelter. It was like that with Kathleen and Sadie. Sadie is like a humming bird darting from one place to another. Benji is calm and relaxed. Sadie dashes. Benji ambles. Benji is gorgeous. Sadie is... well... not.

Until you get to know her.

Now amongst our friends and family she is known as the cutest most lovable ugly dog ever!

She even trumps Benji in the *I-wanna-take-her-home* department.

Because it's still true that you can't judge a book by its cover. Or a dog or a person by the way they look. I often think about what could have happened to Sadie if

Kathleen had not walked into that shelter on that very day and fallen straightaway in love.

At the very least she would've never been on the cover of a book. Which, of course, wouldn't matter to Sadie. Unless somehow she could feel the joy in the smiles that spread across every face I've seen look at the cover of this book. For stirring up joy is why Sadie is on the planet. She considers it her job description.

And a splendid one it is.

"If there are no dogs in Heaven, then when I die,
I want to go where they went."

*Will Rogers*

For more about Joe Camp or pretty much anything in this book please visit one of these sites:

http://thesoulofahorse.com

http://thesoulofahose.com/blog

@joe_camp on Twitter

The Soul of a Horse Channel on Vimeo & YouTube

Joe_Camp & The Soul of a Horse pages on Facebook

Write Joe at
joe@benji.com

www.14handspress.com

Made in the USA
Columbia, SC
05 January 2021

30305132R00064